D0592095

FLOAT LIKE A BUTTERFLY, STING LIKE A BEE

The Wit & Wisdom of Muhammad Ali

FLOAT LIKE A BUTTERFLY, STING LIKE A BEE

The Wit & Wisdom of Muhammad Ali

METRO BOOKS
New York

METRO BOOKS
New York

An Imprint of Sterling Publishing Co., Inc
1166 Avenue of the Americas
New York, NY 10036

Metro Books and the distinctive logo are
registered trademarks of Sterling Publishing

ISBN 978-1-4351-6476-5

For information about custom editions, special sales, and premium
and corporate purchases, please contact Sterling Special Sales at
800-805-5489 or specialsales@sterlingpublishing.com.

Manufactured in China

2 4 6 8 10 9 7 5 3 1

www.sterlingpublishing.com

Designer: Grace Moore
www.graciemagpie.com

Editor: Finn Moore

Cover Design: Lisa Purcell

HE WHO IS NOT **COURAGEOUS** ENOUGH TO TAKE RISKS WILL **ACCOMPLISH NOTHING** IN LIFE.

I AM AN **ORDINARY MAN** WHO WORKED HARD TO DEVELOP THE TALENT I WAS GIVEN...

…I BELIEVED IN MYSELF, AND I BELIEVED IN THE **GOODNESS OF OTHERS**.

IT ISN'T THE MOUNTAINS AHEAD TO CLIMB THAT WEAR YOU OUT; IT'S **THE PEBBLE IN YOUR SHOE.**

SERVICE TO OTHERS IS THE **RENT YOU PAY** FOR YOUR ROOM HERE ON EARTH.

A MAN WHO VIEWS THE WORLD THE SAME AT FIFTY AS HE DID AT TWENTY HAS **WASTED THIRTY YEARS OF HIS LIFE.**

THE MAN WHO HAS NO IMAGINATION **HAS NO WINGS.**

IT IS **LACK OF FAITH** THAT MAKES PEOPLE AFRAID OF MEETING CHALLENGES, AND...

...I BELIEVED
IN MYSELF.

SILENCE IS GOLDEN WHEN YOU CAN'T THINK OF A GOOD ANSWER.

I'VE MADE **MY SHARE OF MISTAKES** ALONG THE WAY, BUT IF I HAVE CHANGED EVEN ONE LIFE FOR THE BETTER, **I HAVEN'T LIVED IN VAIN**.

IMPOSSIBLE IS JUST A BIG WORD THROWN AROUND BY SMALL MEN WHO FIND IT EASIER TO LIVE IN THE WORLD THEY'VE BEEN GIVEN THAN TO EXPLORE THE POWER THEY HAVE TO CHANGE IT. IMPOSSIBLE IS NOT A FACT. IT'S AN OPINION. IMPOSSIBLE IS NOT A DECLARATION. IT'S A DARE. IMPOSSIBLE IS POTENTIAL. IMPOSSIBLE IS TEMPORARY. **IMPOSSIBLE IS NOTHING.**

WARS OF NATIONS ARE FOUGHT TO **CHANGE MAPS**. BUT WARS OF POVERTY ARE FOUGHT TO **MAP CHANGE**.

I WISH PEOPLE WOULD LOVE **EVERYBODY ELSE** THE WAY THEY LOVE ME. IT WOULD BE A **BETTER WORLD.**

IF THEY CAN MAKE
PENICILLIN OUT OF
MOLDY BREAD,
THEY SURE CAN
MAKE SOMETHING
OUT OF YOU.

I'M NOT THE GREATEST; **I'M THE DOUBLE GREATEST.** NOT ONLY DO I KNOCK 'EM OUT, **I PICK THE ROUND.**

TO BE ABLE TO
GIVE AWAY RICHES
IS MANDATORY IF
YOU WISH TO
POSSESS THEM.
THIS IS THE ONLY
WAY THAT YOU WILL
BE TRULY RICH.

WHAT KEEPS ME GOING IS **GOALS.**

AT HOME I AM A NICE GUY: BUT I DON'T WANT THE WORLD TO KNOW. HUMBLE PEOPLE, I'VE FOUND, **DON'T GET VERY FAR.**

I WANTED TO **USE MY FAME, AND THIS FACE** THAT EVERYONE KNOWS SO WELL, TO HELP **UPLIFT AND INSPIRE PEOPLE** AROUND THE WORLD.

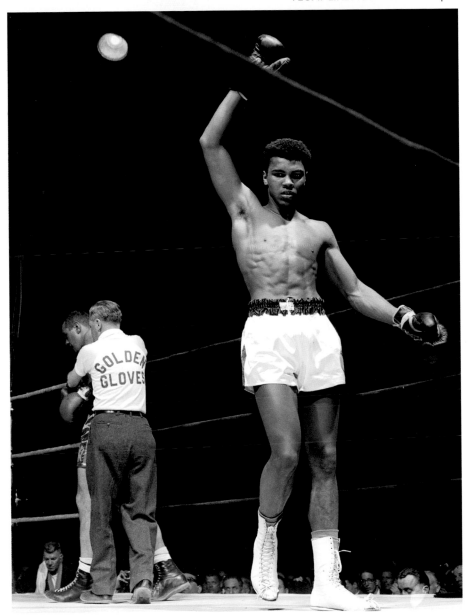

A ROOSTER CROWS ONLY WHEN IT SEES THE LIGHT. PUT HIM IN THE DARK AND HE'LL NEVER CROW. **I HAVE SEEN THE LIGHT, AND I'M CROWING.**

I HATED EVERY MINUTE OF TRAINING, BUT I SAID, "DON'T QUIT. SUFFER NOW AND **LIVE THE REST OF YOUR LIFE AS A CHAMPION."**

FLOAT LIKE A BUTTERFLY, **STING LIKE A BEE!** THE HANDS CAN'T HIT WHAT THE EYES CAN'T SEE.

ONLY A MAN WHO **KNOWS WHAT IT IS LIKE TO BE DEFEATED** CAN REACH DOWN TO THE BOTTOM OF HIS SOUL AND COME UP WITH THE EXTRA OUNCE OF POWER IT TAKES TO WIN **WHEN THE MATCH IS EVEN.**

LIFE IS A GAMBLE. YOU CAN GET HURT, BUT PEOPLE DIE IN PLANE CRASHES, LOSE THEIR ARMS AND LEGS IN CAR ACCIDENTS; PEOPLE DIE EVERY DAY. SAME WITH FIGHTERS: SOME DIE, SOME GET HURT, SOME GO ON. **YOU JUST DON'T LET YOURSELF BELIEVE IT WILL HAPPEN TO YOU.**

LIVE EVERYDAY AS IF IT WERE YOUR LAST BECAUSE SOMEDAY **YOU'RE GOING TO BE RIGHT.**

IF YOU LOSE A BIG FIGHT, IT WILL WORRY YOU ALL OF YOUR LIFE. IT WILL PLAGUE YOU — **UNTIL YOU GET YOUR REVENGE.**

MY TRAINER DON'T
TELL ME NOTHING
BETWEEN ROUNDS.
I DON'T ALLOW HIM TO.
I FIGHT THE FIGHT.
ALL I WANT TO KNOW
IS DID I WIN THE ROUND.
**IT'S TOO LATE
FOR ADVICE.**

NO ONE KNOWS WHAT TO SAY IN THE **LOSER'S LOCKER ROOM.**

MY PRINCIPLES ARE **MORE IMPORTANT** THAN THE MONEY OR MY TITLE.

THERE ARE MORE PLEASANT THINGS TO DO THAN **BEAT UP PEOPLE.**

I BELIEVE IN THE RELIGION OF ISLAM.

I BELIEVE IN ALLAH AND PEACE.

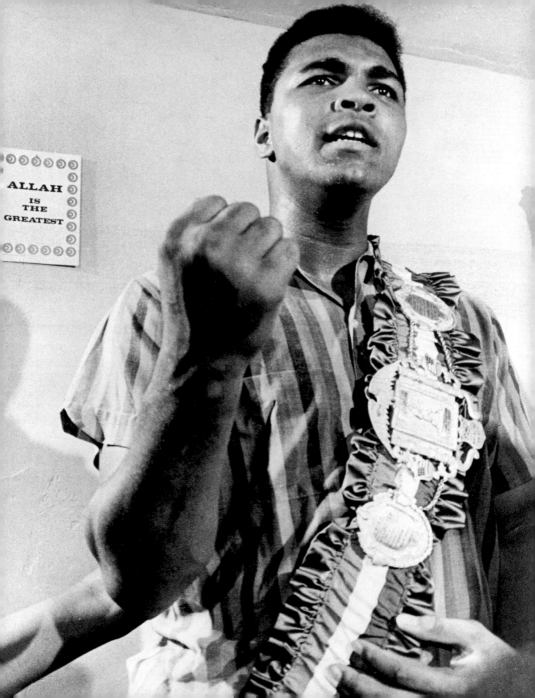

THERE ARE NO PLEASURES IN A FIGHT BUT SOME OF MY FIGHTS HAVE BEEN **A PLEASURE TO WIN.**

I CALCULATE THAT I TOOK **20,000 PUNCHES,** BUT I EARNED MILLIONS AND KEPT A LOT OF IT. I MAY TALK SLOW, BUT **MY MIND IS OK.**

IT'S JUST A JOB.
GRASS GROWS,
BIRDS FLY, WAVES
POUND THE SAND.
I BEAT PEOPLE UP.

AMERICA IS
THE GREATEST
COUNTRY IN
THE WORLD.

BRAGGIN' IS WHEN A PERSON SAYS SOMETHING AND CAN'T DO IT. **I DO WHAT I SAY.**

IT'S **IN MY BLOOD** TO BE AROUND PEOPLE WHILE I WAS TRAINING.

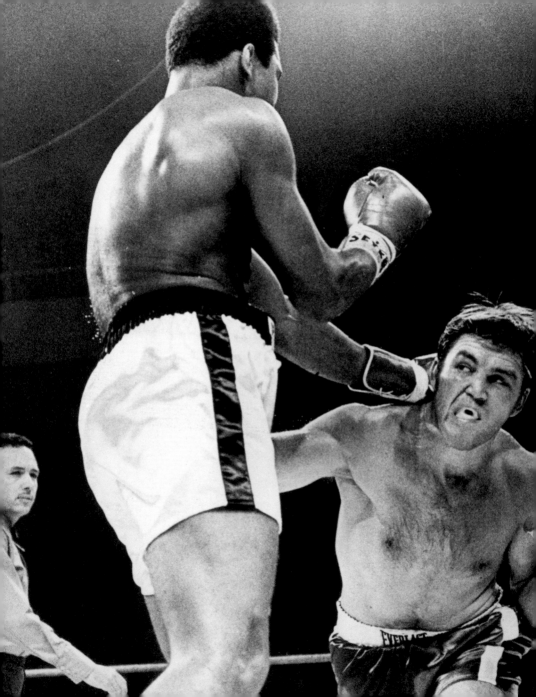

I DONE WRESTED WITH AN ALLIGATOR, I DONE TUSSLED WITH A WHALE; HANDCUFFED LIGHTNING, THROWN THUNDER IN JAIL; ONLY LAST WEEK, I MURDERED A ROCK, INJURED A STONE, HOSPITALIZED A BRICK; **I'M SO MEAN I MAKE MEDICINE SICK.**

IF YOU **EVEN DREAM** OF BEATING ME YOU'D BETTER WAKE UP AND **APOLOGIZE.**

I'M THE GREATEST THING THAT EVER LIVED! **I'M KING OF THE WORLD!** I'M A BAD MAN. I'M THE PRETTIEST THING THAT EVER LIVED.

MY ONLY FAULT IS THAT I DON'T REALIZE JUST **HOW GREAT I REALLY AM.**

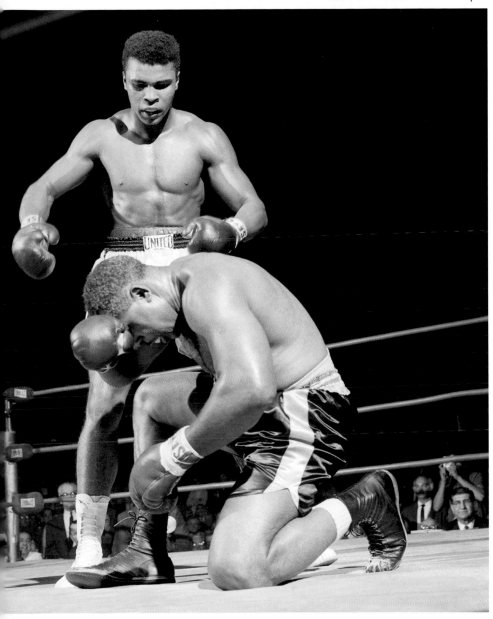

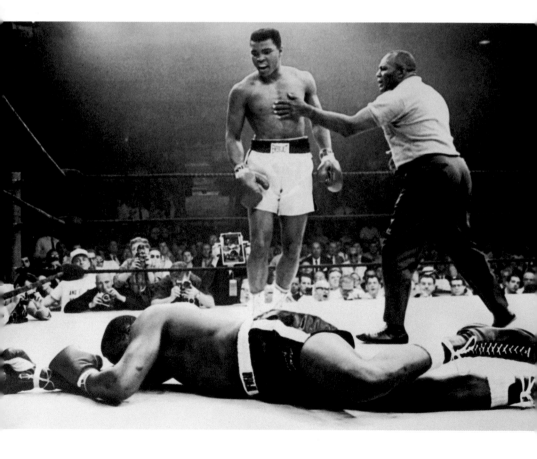

I AM THE GREATEST; I SAID THAT EVEN BEFORE I KNEW I WAS.

DON'T COUNT COUNT
THE DAYS,
**MAKE THE
DAYS COUNT**

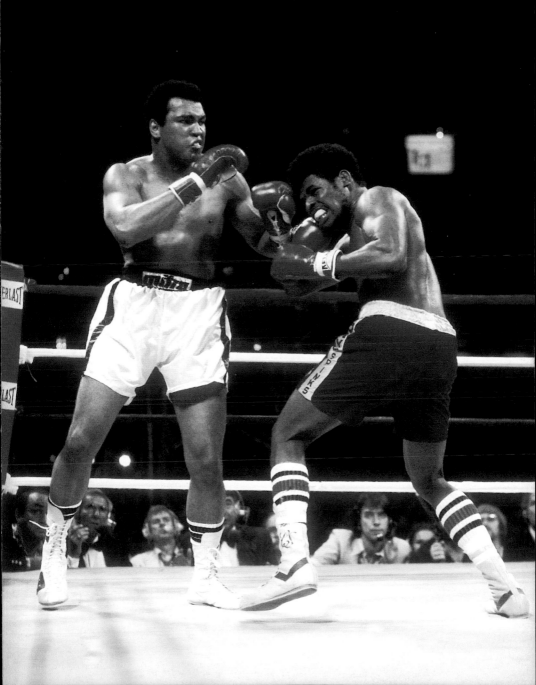

I'VE BEEN EVERYWHERE IN THE WORLD, SEEN EVERYTHING, HAD **EVERYTHING A MAN CAN HAVE.**

I SHOOK UP THE WORLD!

I SHOOK UP THE WORLD!

NEVER PUT YOUR MONEY AGAINST CASSIUS CLAY, FOR YOU WILL NEVER HAVE A **LUCKY DAY.**

IT'S HARD TO BE HUMBLE…

...WHEN YOU'RE AS
GREAT AS I AM.

I SHOULD BE A POSTAGE STAMP, BECAUSE THAT'S THE ONLY WAY I'LL EVER GET LICKED. I'M BEAUTIFUL. I'M FAST. I'M SO MEAN I MAKE MEDICINE SICK…

...I CAN'T POSSIBLY BE BEAT.

I'LL BEAT HIM SO BAD HE'LL NEED A **SHOEHORN** TO PUT HIS HAT ON.

IT WOULD BE A KILLER, AND A CHILLER, AND A THRILLER, WHEN I GET **THE GORILLA IN MANILA.**

THE WORD **"ISLAM"** **MEANS "PEACE,"** THE WORD "MUSLIM" MEANS "ONE WHO SURRENDERS TO GOD." BUT THE PRESS MAKES US SEEM LIKE HATERS.

ALLAH IS THE ARABIC TERM FOR **GOD**…

...STAND UP FOR GOD, FIGHT FOR GOD, WORK FOR GOD AND DO THE RIGHT THING, AND **GO THE RIGHT WAY,** THINGS WILL END UP IN YOUR CORNER.

RIVERS, PONDS, LAKES AND STREAMS - THEY ALL HAVE DIFFERENT NAMES, BUT THEY ALL CONTAIN WATER. JUST AS RELIGIONS DO— THEY ALL CONTAIN **TRUTHS.**

CASSIUS CLAY IS A NAME THAT WHITE PEOPLE GAVE TO MY SLAVE MASTER. **NOW THAT I AM FREE,** THAT I DON'T BELONG ANYMORE TO ANYONE, THAT I'M NOT A SLAVE ANYMORE, I GAVE BACK THEIR WHITE NAME…

...AND I CHOSE
A BEAUTIFUL
AFRICAN ONE.

I WOULD SAY THINGS LIKE "I AM THE GREATEST! I'M PRETTY! IF YOU TALK JIVE, YOU'LL DROP IN FIVE! I FLOAT LIKE A BUTTERFLY, STING LIKE A BEE! I'M PRETTY!" WHEN WHITE PEOPLE HEARD ME TALKING LIKE THIS, SOME SAID, **"THAT BLACK MAN TALKS TOO MUCH. HE'S BRAGGING."**

I HAVE BEEN SO GREAT IN BOXING THEY HAD TO CRE-ATE AN IMAGE LIKE ROCKY, A WHITE IMAGE ON THE SCREEN, TO COUNTER-ACT MY IMAGE IN THE RING. **AMERICA HAS TO HAVE ITS WHITE IMAGES,** NO MATTER WHERE IT GETS THEM: JESUS, WONDER WOMAN, TARZAN AND **ROCKY.**

I KNOW I GOT IT MADE WHILE THE MASSES OF BLACK PEOPLE ARE CATCHIN' HELL, BUT **AS LONG AS THEY AIN'T FREE, I AIN'T FREE.**

BOXING IS A LOT OF WHITE MEN WATCHING TWO BLACK MEN **BEAT EACH OTHER UP.**

HATING PEOPLE BECAUSE OF THEIR COLOR IS WRONG. AND IT DOESN'T MATTER WHICH COLOR DOES THE HATING. **IT'S JUST PLAIN WRONG.**

IT'S NOT BRAGGING IF YOU CAN **BACK IT UP.**

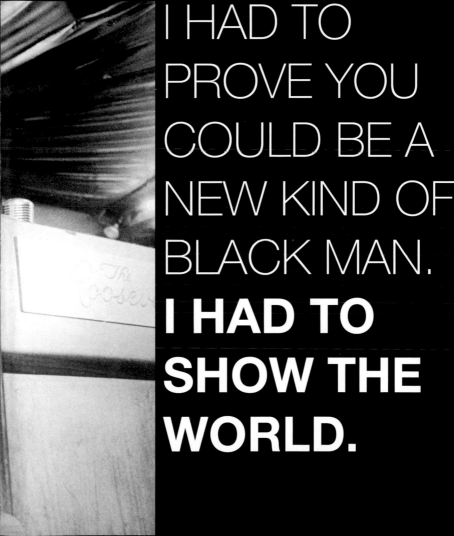

I HAD TO PROVE YOU COULD BE A NEW KIND OF BLACK MAN. **I HAD TO SHOW THE WORLD.**

OLD AGE IS JUST A RECORD OF YOUR **WHOLE LIFE.**

PICTURE CREDITS

All images are by arrangement with Getty Images

Front cover John Shearer; Back cover, top. Central Press; Back cover, bottom. Frank Hurley/*NY Daily News*Archive.

1 John D. Kisch/Separate Cinema Archive; 2 R. McPhedran; 5 Central Press / Stringer; 7 Bettmann; 8 Popperfoto; 11 Neil Leifer; 12 Bettmann; 14 James Drake; 17 AFP / Stringer; 19 B. Potter / Stringer; 20 Terry O'Neill; 23 Tony Duffy / AllSport; 24 Marvin Lichtner; 27 James Drake; 28 Express / Stringer; 31 Bettman; 33 Popperfoto John Shearer; 36 Central Press / Stringer; 39 Popperfoto; 41 Frank Hurley/*NY Daily News* Archive; 42 Enrico Sarsini; 45 Bettmann; 46 Focus on Sport; 49 Rolls Press/Popperfoto; 50 Pierre Boulat; 52 John Shearer; 55 Ron Galella/WireImage; 56 Focus on Sport; 59 Chris Smith/Popperfoto; 60 Popperfoto; 62 Herb Scharfman; 65 Bob Gomel; 66 Keystone; 69 Rolls Press; 70 Neil Leifer; 73 Central Press; 74 Herb Scharfman; 77 R. McPhedran; 78 Keystone; 81 Central Press; 82–3 Popperfoto; 84–5 Hy Peskin; 86 Agence France Presse; 89 Manny Millan; 91 *NY Daily News* Archive / Anthony Casale; 92–3 Allsport Hulton/Archive; 94 Allsport Hulton/Archive; 96–7 Les Lee; 99. Art Rickerby; 100 Mark Kauffman; 103 Dieter Ludwig; 104 Tony Tomsic; 106 David Fenton; 108 Popperfoto; 111 AFP; 112 R. McPhedran; 115 Rolls Press/Popperfoto; 116–7 Gerry Cranham/Sports Illustrated; 119 Focus on Sport; 120 Herb Scharfman/Sports Imagery; 123 Keystone; 124 Bill Meurer/*NY Daily News* Archive; 127 Jeff Kowalsky